# B )F

# OLD RINGWOOD

By
Mary Baldwin

Designed and Illustrated by
Terry Hood-Cree

**PUBLISHED BY**
**RINGWOOD BREWERY**



ISBN 0 9516861 0 0
PRINTED BY PARDY & SON (PRINTERS) LTD., RINGWOOD, HAMPSHIRE

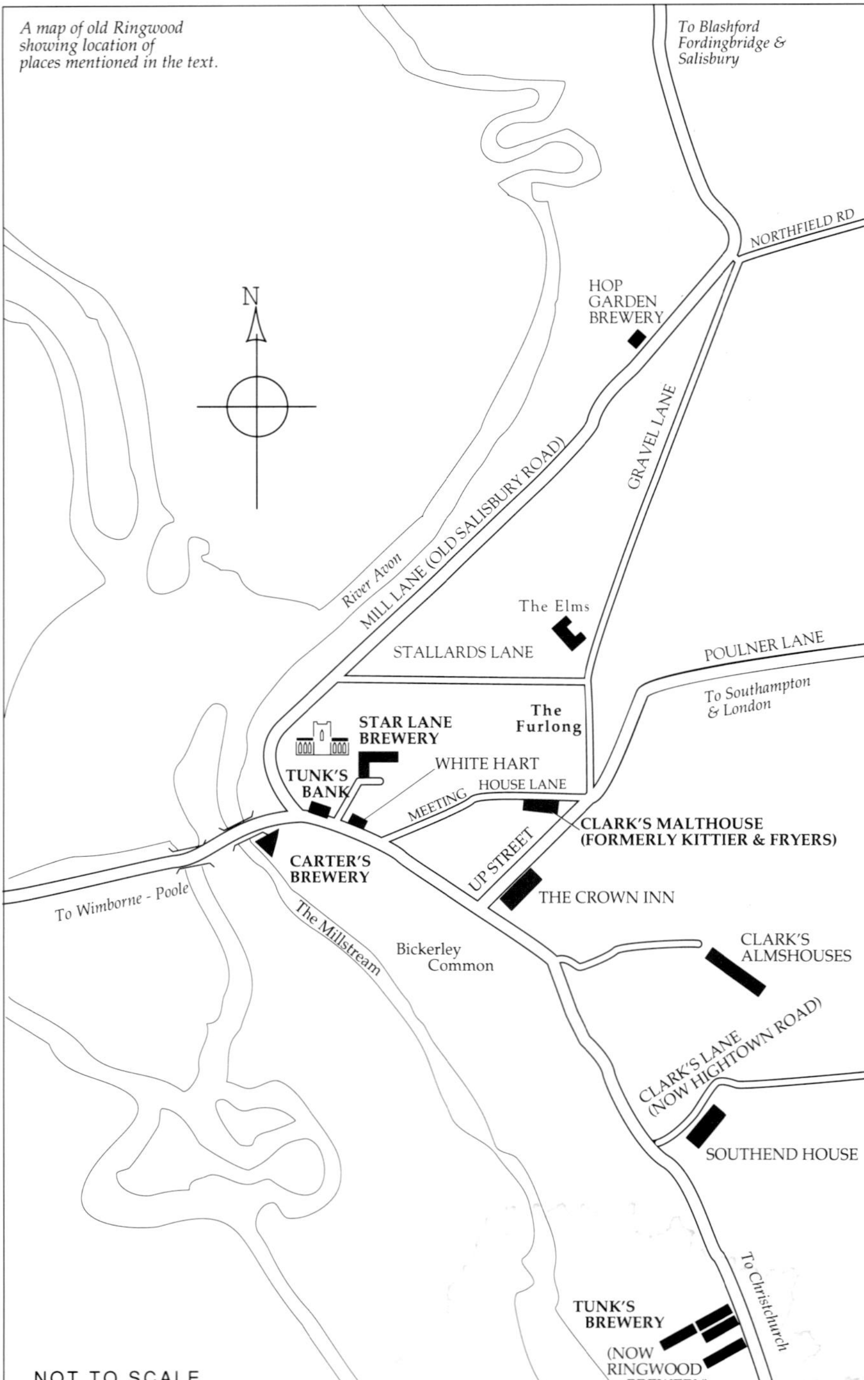
A map of old Ringwood showing location of places mentioned in the text.
To Blashford Fordingbridge & Salisbury
N
NORTHFIELD RD
HOP GARDEN BREWERY
GRAVEL LANE
MILL LANE (OLD SALISBURY ROAD)
River Avon
The Elms
STALLARDS LANE
POULNER LANE
To Southampton & London
The Furlong
STAR LANE BREWERY
WHITE HART
TUNK'S BANK
MEETING HOUSE LANE
CLARK'S MALTHOUSE (FORMERLY KITTIER & FRYERS)
CARTER'S BREWERY
UP STREET
THE CROWN INN
To Wimborne - Poole
The Millstream
Bickerley Common
CLARK'S ALMSHOUSES
CLARK'S LANE (NOW HIGHTOWN ROAD)
SOUTHEND HOUSE
To Christchurch
TUNK'S BREWERY
(NOW RINGWOOD BREWERY)
NOT TO SCALE

# INTRODUCTION

Ask any elderly life-long resident of Ringwood and they will tell you that Ringwood is not the same town they knew as a child. Then they could reckon to know the names of most people they met in the street, the shops were all run by local families and a motor car in the High Street was an occasional novelty not a continual hazard. The impression they fondly leave is of a pleasant, some would say sleepy, self-contained little back-water.

Yet two hundred years ago, before the spectacular growth of Bournemouth in Victorian times, Ringwood had been a busy centre of administrative importance. As well as a weekly market serving a wide agricultural area, Ringwood had also once boasted traditional industries such as cloth-making, stocking and glove-knitting, tanning, milling and brewing. Of these, brewing was considered the most important, for Ringwood was famous far and wide for the high reputation of its ales.

Situated on the western edge of the New Forest in Hampshire, at a crossing point of the River Avon, Ringwood has a history dating back to before the time of the Domesday Book. By 1811 its population was reckoned to be 3269, according to contemporary census figures. The town was one of the largest in the district, capable of sustaining three coaching inns, (The White Hart, Crown, and Red Lion), plus at least thirteen other inns in its centre, (The Fish, Antelope, New, George, Royal Oak, Star, White Lion, King's Arms, Rose & Crown, Compton Arms, Smith's Arms, Lamb and King's Head.) Besides these, there were many others on the outskirts of town.

By the close of the 19th century, however, the town's relative importance had declined. A.H.Kingsbury, writing in 1894, had to remind his readers that in the days before the railway, *'the direct road between Poole and London lay through Ringwood; and a large amount of traffic between Salisbury and the coast, and Southampton and the west passed through the town.... The great carrier waggons daily rumbled along the highways, and we may be sure all the drivers stopped to have a long and deep draught of old Ringwood's famous ale, so altogether the town must have had a more busy and bustling appearance than at the present day.'*

It was this busier period, roughly between the start of the reign of

George 111 in 1760 and that of Queen Victoria in 1837, that can be regarded as the heyday of the common brewer in Ringwood. At that time Ringwood was said to have swarmed with malthouses and breweries. There were so many that to attempt to identify them all would be a virtual impossibility. The following account aims to describe only something of the lives and times of the most well-known brewers in that era before the railway and camera.Time has snatched away all but the barest memories of those days, so much research has been needed to try to recapture their details. In particular, this account contains a great deal of hitherto undiscovered information obtained from contemporary copies of the Salisbury & Winchester Journal and from original documents deposited at the Hampshire Record Office.

The typescript by the late Dr. Little on Ringwood breweries has provided an invaluable starting-point for this research. I would also like to acknowledge the kind co-operation I have received from the Salisbury Journal, the staff of all the library and museum services at Ringwood, Salisbury, Poole, Christchurch and Winchester, and the many other people who have helped, particularly my fellow-members of the Local History Workshop Group. Finally I am very grateful to David Welsh, the Managing Director of today's Ringwood Brewery, for his enthusiasm and commitment in backing the entire project.

Mary R. Baldwin August 1990

# BREWERS OF OLD RINGWOOD

Brewing in England has a history going back at least to Roman times. By the Middle Ages the brewing of ale, using only the ingredients barley, water and yeast, was well established.

Firstly the barley was made into malt by a process of soaking and then drying. The malt was crushed and mixed with hot water to produce a sweet solution—this was boiled and cooled before yeast was added to complete the brewing, most of which was done at home.

It was quite common during this period for both the brewing and retailing of ale to be carried out by women. H.A. Monckton in 'A History of English Ale and Beer' quotes a number of cases of medieval brewsters and ale-wives being charged with fraudulent practices, for which the punish ment was often the ducking-stool or the stocks. A dishonest ale-wife with a jug in her hand, being carried away by a devil, is portrayed locally in the famous medieval 'Doom' painting on the chancel arch of St.Thomas's Church, Salisbury. The Lord of the Manor, through the Court Leet, would have appointed an ale-taster to check up on any such dishonesty, but this job was probably not as attractive as it sounds!

It is very likely that Church-Ales would have been a popular event in medieval Ringwood. These ales were brewed at certain times of the year, especially Whitsun, by the churchwardens and sold to parishioners. Profits went towards the upkeep of the Church.

During the 15th century, beer, which contained hops, was first introduced to this country from Holland. The hops added flavour and lengthened the life of the beer. The following poem of 1577 recommended the use of hops to the brewer:

> 'The hop for his profit I thus do exalt,
> It strengthenth drink and it flavoureth malt;
> And being well-brewed long kept it will last,
> And drawing abide, if ye draw not too fast.'

Although Henry VIII made a vain attempt to forbid the brewing of beer as opposed to ale, it was gradually accepted alongside ale and by the

18th century the two terms were more or less synonymous.

In former times beer, along with bread and cheese, was of the greatest importance in the diet of every ordinary man, woman and child. A.H. Kingsbury in his 'History of Ringwood' wrote: *'Such foreign beverages as tea and coffee were great luxuries, and ale was the drink that braced a man at the outset of his day's toil and refreshed him at its close... Ringwood at one time seemed almost all breweries and malthouses. The public taste for beer was then different from now; a strong heavy liquor was loved, and tastes were not too squeamish, even the water from a horsepond was held excellent for brewing, and the leaves of bog-myrtle, so common in the Forest, were often used in the place of hops.'*

Although this does not sound very pleasant, it must be remembered that good ale or beer was sterilized in the making and was thus safer than water, which was often contaminated and contained nothing in the way of nourishment. Beer was therefore considered more as an essential rather than a luxury. It was not until the latter half of the 19th century that the temperance movement and the availability of tea at an affordable price as an alternative, brought about changes in people's drinking habits.

Beer varied in strength; men usually drank strong beer, whereas women and children often drank a weaker brew known as small beer. Small beer, like water, was not considered as safe as strong. A gravestone at Winchester recording the death in 1764 of a soldier named Thomas Thetcher, laid the blame for his violent fever on his drinking small beer when hot, and added the following warning:

> *'Here sleeps in peace a Hampshire Grenadier*
> *Who caught his death by drinking cold small Beer*
> *Soldiers be wise from his untimely fall*
> *And when ye're hot drink Strong or none at all.*

The amount of beer drunk by men doing hard physical work was considerable. One particular man named Bower, a gardener from Blashford who cared for the trees in Ringwood churchyard in the mid-18th century, was noted as *'a man remarkable fond of good ale, particularly that sold at the George.'* He was said to have drunk sixteen pints a day when at work in the churchyard, allowing the Sexton a half-pint to every pint he drank himself!

Although much brewing was still carried out by women at home and on the farm, the malting of barley and the commercial brewing and retailing of beer had become mainly a masculine trade by the 18th century. Retailers often still brewed on or near their premises. For example, an advertisement of 1795 for a new tenant of the White Hart Inn in Ringwood Market Place, specifically stated that *"The occupier will be at liberty to brew his own beer.'* When Ringwood Friendly Society celebrated their anniversary in June 1822, Mr. Edward Brickell (or Bicknell), the landlord of the Red Lion, provided *'home-made stingo which gave general satisfaction, being reduced in price and increased in strength'.* (Stingo was a slang name for strong beer.)

The waters of the River Avon and plentiful supplies of local barley made Ringwood an ideal site for commercial brewing. Hops were grown locally, particularly at Poulner. Ringwood also had its market every Wednesday, when barley was bought and sold and no doubt a great quantity of the end product was consumed! The following advertisement shows that a wide range of brewing utensils was quite likely to be included among other everyday goods sold on Market-Day:

'26th November 1794. *For sale by auction in the Market-Place at Ringwood - A copper furnace which contains 100 gallons, an Iron Grate, a deal vat for making 18 bushels, two coolers, an under-back, a four-hogshead cask, 11 iron-bound pipes, a puncheon, four half-hogsheads, two water casks, brewing and washing tubs, a cucumber-frame with three lights, garden roller, a rick of meadow hay, an old post-chaise, two pairs of hind chaise wheels and numerous other items.'*

Also for sale by private contract were: '*a good Brewing Copper (contains 180 gallons), a round mash vat, wood under-back, three coolers and two lead liquor-pumps, the whole complete for brewing five quarters of malt.'*

The capacity of these items suggests that they may have been for commercial rather than domestic use and so were probably bought by one of the many common brewers in Ringwood.

Although by no means a comprehensive list, the first directory to include Ringwood, published in 1784, gave the names of five brewers and brewing companies - Merryweather & Neave, Wm Clark & Co., Samuel Scutt, Joseph Veal, and Tunks & Sweetland.

The partnership of Merryweather & Neave involved two men from well-known local families, John Merryweather of Ringwood and Josiah

Neave Jnr. of Fordingbridge. The only information on their brewery indicates that by 1784 it had in fact been sold:

*'August 25th 1783 - To be sold and entered upon at Michaelmas next, a BREWERY with or without a large Malthouse, conveniently situated at Blashford, where an extensive trade has been for many years carried on, and for which the premises are well adapted. The purchaser may also be accommodated with two well-accustomed public houses.*

*NB. A large number of hogshead and other casks with various other utensils in the brewing trade, to be disposed of.'*

The directory was also a little out of date with its information on Clark & Co. William Clark and his partner Sarah Stephens had been declared bankrupt in 1783 and the following property put up for auction:

*'July 14th 1783 - All that messuage, tenement or dwellinghouse with the Brewhouse, Malthouse, Millhouse, stable, cellars and several pieces of ground, situate lying and being at Hop Garden, in the parish of Ringwood, late in the occupation of Sarah Stephens.*

*N.B. On the premises a considerable brewery was lately carried on, and the same was very commodious and fit for that trade.'*

Hop Garden (itself an interesting indication of the local cultivation of hops) was an area on the Avon side of the old Salisbury Road as shown on a map of 1769. There is no further record of a brewery there after 1783. On the 1847 tithe map a house and yards belonging to timber-merchant Charles Sharp are shown as occupying this site, also known as Spring Gardens. This house is now called Avon Glen, but the deeds of the cottage next door still refer to the area as Hop Garden.

The next brewer in the 1784 directory was Samuel Scutt. His brewery was situated in West Street now the site of the bus depot next to the Millstream. The small brick bridge over the Millstream is still known locally as Scutt's Bridge.

It has been repeatedly stated that this brewery was founded in 1725 by Alexander Carter. However, documents deposited at Hampshire Record Office now prove this claim to be incorrect. In fact it was a man named Benjamin Bound who first built the brewery, malthouse and three large cellars on what had previously been a tannery. (Tanyards in 18th century Ringwood were almost as numerous as breweries!)

Samuel Scutt acquired the brewery by marrying Bound's daughter Mary. In turn Alexander Carter eventually came into possession of the brewery through his marriage to Samuel and Mary Scutt's only child, Elizabeth. In 1802, seventeen years after Alexander and Elizabeth's marriage, Samuel Scutt agreed to transfer to them all his property, valued at over £4000, on condition that he and his wife were paid an annuity for life.

Alexander Carter made many changes to his newly-acquired property. Not only did he refurbish the brewery with new utensils and fixtures, by 1812 he had pulled down Scutt's old house which had adjoined it, and erected a new dwelling-house for himself and his large family. This is the elegant Georgian building known as Bridge House, now Armfields Technical Education offices. Carter also demolished the public-house next door called 'The Waggon & Horses', and put in its place a new one named 'The Antelope' (now part of Ringwood Social Club). It may also have been Alexander who installed in the brewery the famous huge 5000 gallon vat, inside which parties were later said to have taken place!

Alexander and Elizabeth Carter had eight surviving children, three boys and five girls. Their eldest son and heir was Samuel London Carter, who in March 1822 surprisingly put the entire brewery, house and the Antelope Inn up to be sold or let. The details advertised in the Salisbury Journal emphasized its prime location:

*'The Brewery in point of situation and convenience is perhaps surpassed by few; it adjoins a most delightful stream of water from which the Brewery is constantly supplied'.*

Perhaps this was part of some legal means whereby Samuel sold his inheritance to another member of the family, for the premises definitely remained in the Carter family after Samuel London Carter moved to Poole and subsequently died.

In 1834 his younger brother Alexander set up in partnership with his sisters Sarah, Caroline and Jane, trading under the name 'Alexander Carter & Co.' (Presumably the youngest brother, named Benjamin Bound Carter in honour of his illustrious great-grandfather, had died.) Relations between Alexander and his sisters were not always happy; at one point ill-feelings between them over the way Alexander ran the brewery were so bad that an outsider had to be called in to act as a sort of legal umpire! On one matter, however, they were in complete agreement - the Carters were all staunch supporters of the Congregational Church (now Trinity United Reform). In 1863 they donated the land in Christchurch Road on which the present Trinity Church was built.

On Alexander's death in 1869, the business passed to his sister Sarah Carter who, strangely for a brewery-owner, was a keen promoter of temperance! She was even known to distribute temperance tracts amongst her employees! Miss Carter was also a generous benefactress of the town, building and endowing the since-demolished Lecture Hall in Christchurch Road, on the stipulation that no alcohol was to be drunk on the premises. Here is a good example of the dichotomy which began to confront non-conformist brewers as the Victorian temperance movement gained strength. Earlier Georgian brewers saw no such conflict between their religious and commercial practices.

When Sarah died the brewery was left to her nephew Reginald Jennings, who came from Australia to claim his inheritance. This gentleman was said to have always worn a top-hat and frock-coat and, although looking very forbidding with his long black beard, was full of 'good works'. Mr Jennings was the great, great-grandson of Benjamin Bound, so the brewery had passed down five generations of the same family. However, because of the female line of descent, only two generations actually bore the name Carter, the name by which the brewery became famous.

*The Brewer*

The brewery was eventually sold out of the Carter family in 1887, and passed to a Joseph Shuttleworth of Northampton. Miss Shuttleworth married the manager of the brewery, Mr. Howard Tozer of Leybrook Lodge, Ashley, who for many years was also churchwarden of the Parish Church. (Control of this brewery seems to have continually involved marrying the owner's daughter!) Carter's famous name was retained and their popular ales continued to be brewed in West Street. In Brown's Ringwood Almanac, Carter's specialities were advertised as 'Double Invalid Stout at 1/6d per gallon and A.K., a bright pleasant light bitter Dinner Ale at 1/- per gallon.' The advertisement's claim that the brewery was founded in 1725 cannot be correct, as Benjamin Bound did not acquire the tanyard site until 1741!

According to Mr. Ted Rogers, who worked as a grocer's errand boy during the 1st World War, Mr.Tozer used to send foodparcels including items such as Oxo cubes, out to members of his staff who had joined the Forces. One of these men was Royal Engineer Charlie Withall, the cooper. Other employees included Mr Kirby the Head Brewer, Alfred Still the cellar man, Jim Wareham the dray-man, and Roley Thomas, who drove Mr.Tozer around in a horse and cart to collect orders.

The brewery finally closed in 1923, having been bought out by Strong's of Romsey. The large vat was dismantled and brewing in Ringwood ceased. There then followed a regrettable lapse of over fifty years until 1978, when today's Ringwood Brewery was founded by Mr. Peter Austin, and Ringwood's traditional reputation for strong ale was re-established.

Returning to the directory of 1784, the fourth brewer mentioned was Joseph Veal. He rented the brewery at the top of Star Lane owned by a family named Marten. Quite possibly this was the oldest brewery in Ringwood; evidence suggests that in the 17th century it had belonged to the influential Lyne family. With the brewery went the tenancies of the Star and the White Lion (now W.Ayles shop), both situated in the nearby Market Place. Water, a fundamental necessity for any brewery, was conveyed from the Millpond on the nearby River Avon *'through a pipe or drain lately made by Stephen Marten.'*

On his son's marriage in 1790, Joseph Veal, like Samuel Scutt, agreed to surrender his brewing business, valued at over £2000, entirely over to his son. Unfortunately the son, Joseph Veal Jnr, died at an early age in 1801, leaving his young widow Elizabeth with three small children. In his will Joseph Veal Jnr expressed the wish that Elizabeth should carry on the brewery, advised and assisted by his father and his friends Thomas and William Clark. The latter was to become more than just a good friend, for two years later William Clark married Elizabeth Veal and took over the running of her brewery.

William Clark, whose life spanned from 1763 to 1841, was one of Ringwood's most influential citizens of the early 19th century. He does not appear to be any relation of the earlier Clark who went bankrupt in 1783. William was the second son of a wealthy and respectable merchant from Poole named Thomas Clark, who lived at Southend House in what was then Clark's Lane, now Hightown Road. (A later occupier of this house, Stephen Ayles, is known to have brewed beer there in Victorian times. For many years the words 'Ayles Ales' could be seen painted on the side of the house.)

For two decades Clark continued to run the brewery for the benefit of his three step-children, under the name of 'Veal & Company' in accordance with the wishes of their father. It had been Veal's hope that his elder son, John Bessant Veal, would take over the business when he became of age, but the boy had other ideas and declined to be brought up in the trade, preferring to go to sea in His Majesty's Service. Did he, perhaps, take part as a young midshipman in the Battle of Trafalgar?

In 1822 Clark wrote to the owner of the brewery, Mrs. Marten, to complain about the state of the property:

*'The premises are in want of thatch, and the dwelling-house is much out of repair that it rains in very much which will injure the ceilings and floor if not attended to..... the present rent which we now give is so much out of all bounds that it is impossible to continue it at any such rate.'*

Clark evidently managed to get his reduction in rent as in 1823 he renewed the lease at a lower rent of £90 per annum. By this time he and his wife Elizabeth had bought out the shares of the remaining two Veal children, and from then on the business was run in the name of Clark, with William always regarding this business as his wife's.

By 1840 the owner of the brewery had become William Newton Parsons, who let it to an Isaac Veal, later to be joined by his son Frederic. These Veals may have been cousins of the earlier Veal family, but the surname was then a common one in Ringwood, so it is difficult to be sure. Isaac and Frederic Veal, like the Carters, were great supporters of Trinity Church. Frederic is commemorated by a tablet inside the church, which records that he was a lifelong worshipper, deacon and Church Secretary. Later in the century the brewery passed into the hands of Messrs Panton of Wimborne. It is believed to have closed in 1893, having been bought out by Strong's of Romsey, thus leaving only Carters to survive into the 20th century.

The house that went with the brewery, mentioned by Clark as out of repair, still stands at the top of Star Lane. Now known as Lynton House, it has a late Victorian addition to the front and many other alterations. For many years this century it was the home of members of the Frampton family, after the brewery buildings became their corn stores. Nobody seems to be quite certain of the actual date Framptons acquired the yard, but it was probably around 1893, soon after the closure of the brewery.

The evidence from Clark's letter that the brewery was originally thatched is confirmed by Mr. Stan Vowles, who worked in Frampton's Yard for many years. He can recall being told in the early 1960s by a Mr.Hoare (then aged over 80), that as a young lad one of Mr.Hoare's first jobs was to take the thatch off the old malt-house (which became

*West Street, Carter's Brewery and Scutt's Bridge can be seen on the right hand side*

Frampton's office), so that it could be slated. According to information given to Mr. Vowles by the late Mr.Alec Frampton, the popular three - storeyed building known as 'Frampton's Mill' was built about 1913, and is therefore of a much later date than the original L-shaped brewery buildings it adjoined. This whole site is now being redeveloped as part of the Furlong Shopping Complex.

William Clark in his own right also owned the malthouse which ranged along the south side of Meeting House Lane, from the Meeting House to Up street (now Southampton Rd). This property had once belonged to two brewers named Kittier & Fryer as shown on a map of 1769.

Some idea of the output of this brewery can be gained from the account books of William Ayles, a local carrier who delivered beer to various places such as Poole, Southampton, Lymington and Salisbury. In a single year, October 1764-1765, he carried some 197 hogsheads (over 10,000 gallons) for Joseph Fryer.

*The Maltster*

It was by more than mere chance that the prosperity of Ringwood's breweries during the late 18th century coincided with the golden age of Poole, Dorset. Poole was not far from Ringwood down the comparatively good turnpike road and there was money to be made supplying all kinds of goods to the cod fishers of Newfoundland via this port. For instance, it was through ship-owning and Newfoundland trading that the Clark family had acquired their considerable wealth. Brewers Moses Kittier and Joseph Fryer were also both involved in the Newfoundland trade. One can imagine the many casks of Ringwood beer that must have made the rough crossing over the Atlantic from Poole to satisfy the thirst of those intrepid Newfoundland planters!

Fortunes could be lost as well as gained however, and troubles lay ahead. On the night of July 23rd 1772, the brewhouse of Kittier & Fryer was *'maliciously set on fire by some wicked and ill-designed person or persons.'* A reward of fifty guineas was offered for information leading to the conviction of the offenders, half to be paid by the brewers and the other half by inhabitants of the town. Apparently the arsonists went undetected, for other fires, including one in an outhouse of the White Hart Inn, continued with *'great reason to suppose they have not all been occasioned by accident.'*

Despite this, and a further set-back when his former partner Moses Kittier was declared bankrupt in 1780, Joseph Fryer must have rebuilt his brewery and continued the business until 1786:

May 29 1786. *To be sold or let - All that well-known Brewhouse and Malthouse, with convenient buildings, almost new, and in compleat repair, exceedingly well-adapted for carrying on an extensive trade, now in the hands of the owner, Joseph Fryer, who is going to retire from that branch of the business. A small stock of good old Strong Beer, and all the utensils, empty casks etc., may be taken at a fair appraisement.'*

His imminent retirement may have been the reason why Fryer was not included in the 1784 directory. Possibly the brewery was then rented by Richard Gibbs, owner of the nearby White Hart Inn until 1795, as Fryer's will, dated 3rd January 1798, refers to *'all that messuage, tenement or dwellinghouse, malthouse, outbuildings etc, called Gibbs, now in my possession'.*

When Fryer eventually died in 1802, the brewery was again put up for sale. Whether it was then or later that Clark acquired this property is unknown, but the town tithe map made four years after Clark's death clearly shows that the premises, by then vacant and later demolished, belonged to his widow Elizabeth Clark. The main entrance to the brewery yard must then have fronted on to Southampton Road, somewhere near what is now Woolworth's. At that time of course, all traffic travelling between London and Poole had to pass along Up Street, the old name for Southampton Road, so this brewery had a good location. Its only drawback must have been that it was not next to the river; presumably it must have used wells, unless water was piped from the Millpond, as was the Star Lane Brewery.

William Clark was a meticulous businessman who kept detailed accounts of all his transactions which give an interesting insight into his trade. For instance, although hops were grown locally and also at Farnham, he purchased only the best hops from Kent, as is shown by this letter:

*'Messrs Bush & White 21 June 1814 Gentlemen, Will you please send me down a pockett of good Kent hops by Artlett's first waggon do not fail sending them as I think I shall be in want by the time they arrive.'*

A pocket is the special name given to a sack of hops. Alas, deliveries were a problem as is clear from his next letter:

*'Messrs Bush & White 29 August814*

*The purport of my now writing is to say that Artlett's waggon is arrived here from London and the pockett of Hops you last sent is not come, should thank you to get them forwarded by the next opportunity which will be tomorrow or next day, that if they do not come then we shall be destitute.'*

Barley was bought locally - Clark's accounts show large amounts being delivered to his maltster William Langor in Up Street. Clark

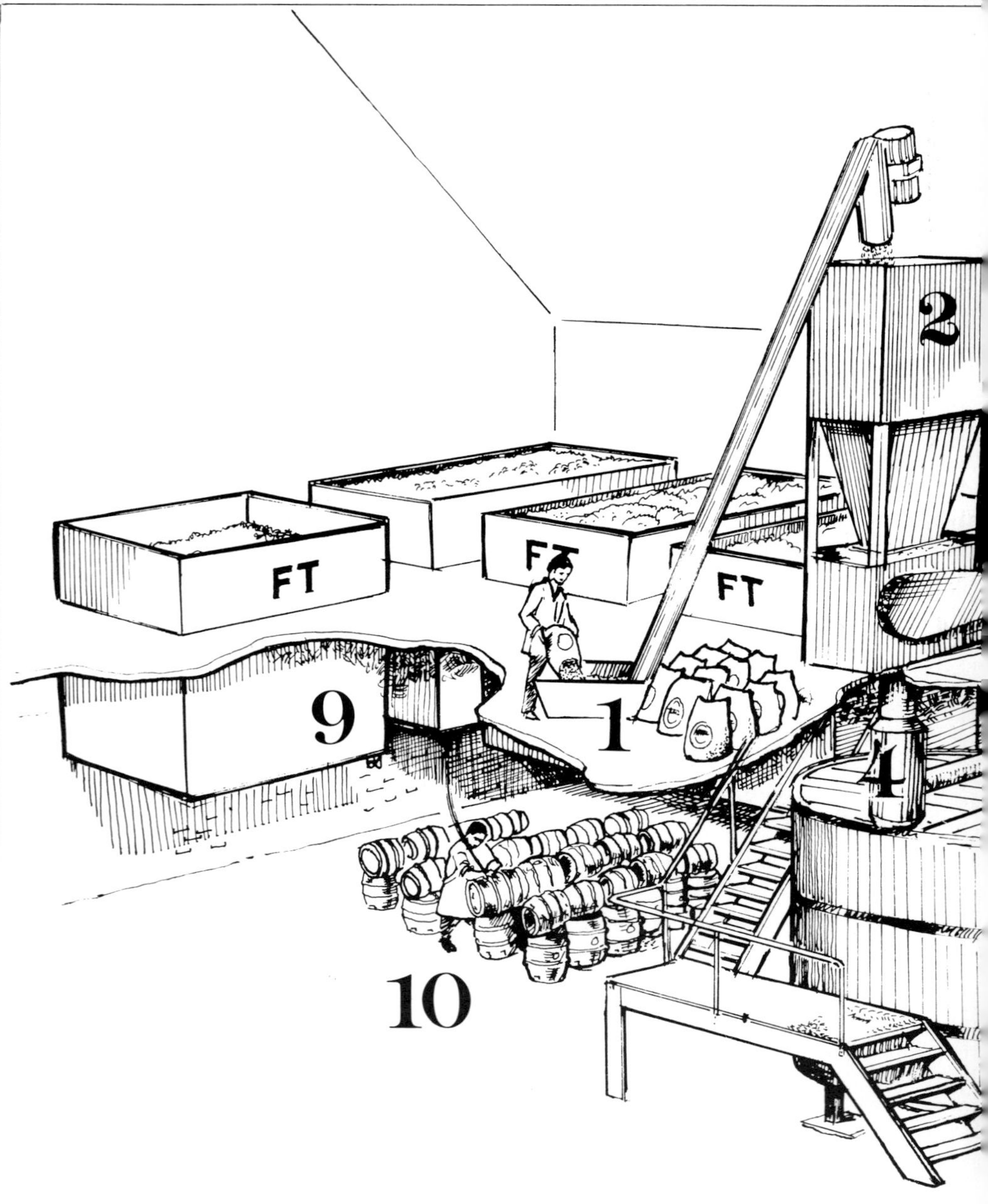


1. MALT
2. MILL
3. HOT LIQUOR BACK
4. MASHER
5. MASH TUN
6. COPPER WHIRL POOL
7. CALANDRIA
8. HOPS
9. FERMENTING TUNS
10. RACKING HALL

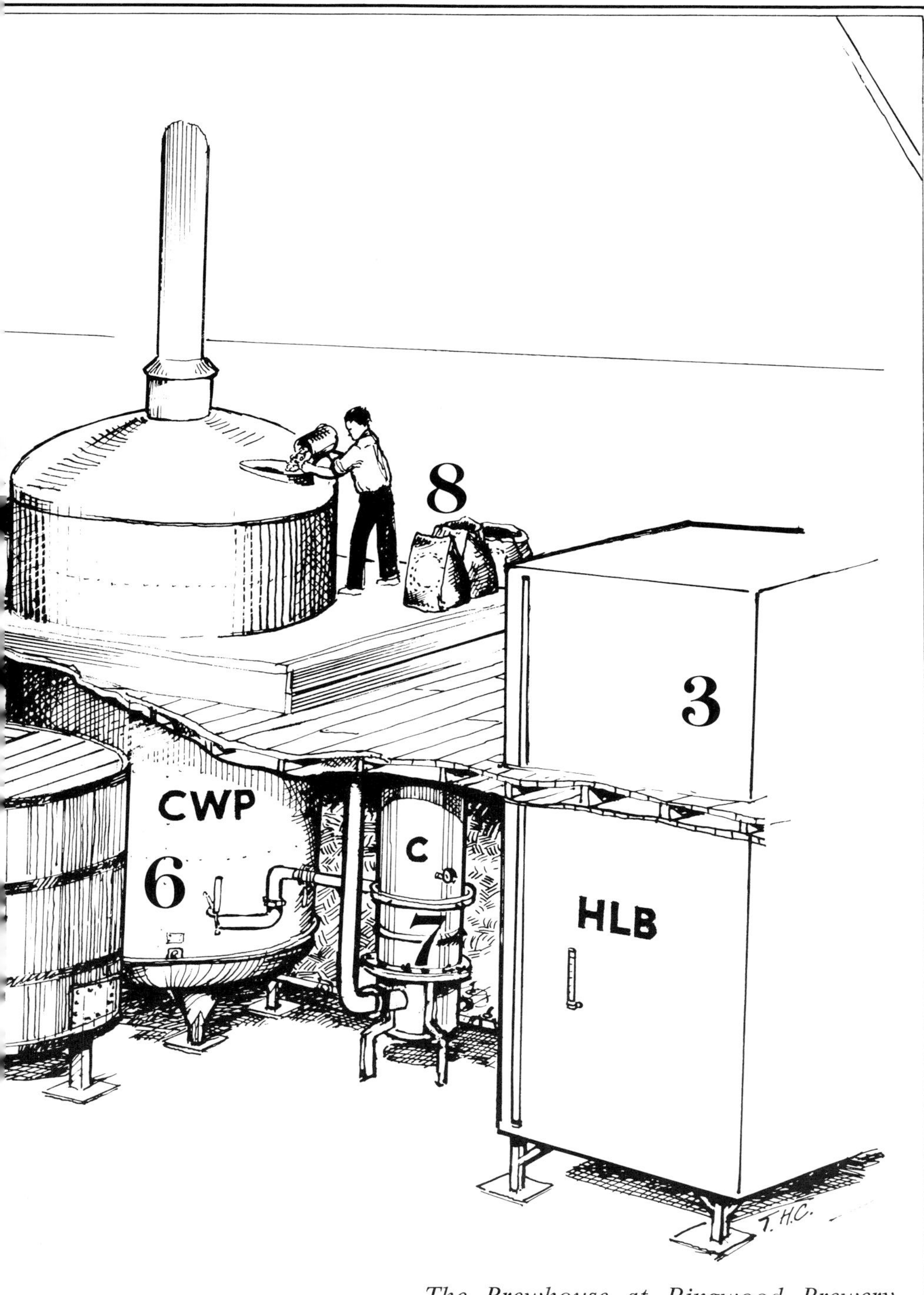


*The Brewhouse at Ringwood Brewery*

himself was responsible for the buying of the barley, which he bought in the Market Place every Wednesday. This again involved him in difficulties, as did spelling and grammar!:

*'Mr. J Newman, Kingstone 2nd May 1822*

*When I went to the Malthouse and seen the Barly you sent in yesterday I was very much surprised. How could you have acted in such a manner to sell me Barly by a remarkable good sample which I have by me now, and send in such inferior quality, so much different from it, that I have not seen anything so bad a Load this year. I have sent a man for to call on you and bring some empty sacks to measure it back again and should wish you to come for it as soon as you can, and inform him what day as it will be in our way.'*

*'Mr. Newman 29 May 1822*

*I have expected to have seen you at our Market this two following weeks as agreed, but being disappointed is the occasion of my now writing and I have to say, should be glad if you would send for your Barly which is at our Malthouse.'*

Even when the beer had been made, there could still be problems:

*'Mr. Panton 25 February 1817*

*We have met with a disappointment in filling our large cask after having put into it about 140 barrells it leak't and was forced to take it all out again and it must remain empty.'*

Another letter shows yet more problems that could occur once the beer had been casked:

*Mr. T.N.Robilliard 6 Nov. 1816*

*Dear Sir*

*If it was in my power to assist you with any remedy to bring your Beer which have turned Sour to its sound state and sweetness, it would have given me great pleasure, but I know nothing affectually that will do it, it depends how far it is gone; if not to sour, mixing some fresh new Beer with Hops may bring it round, but if too far gone it will be only adding more loss. I have known Beer that have turned acid, but it have been well Malted, that is to say made strong, by keeping it a length of time, have made excellent vinigar - yours may do the same, and if I found it get no better I would try a small cask, and put it out into the open air where the Sun can well come at it, and see where* [whether] *it would make vinegar that way, but I have known it come to good vinigar in the same cask in the cellar by keeping. You may try both ways.'*

Despite all these difficulties, the industrious Mr. Clark prospered, and sometime after 1820 purchased 'The Elms', a fine Georgian house near the Furlong which was demolished in 1978 to make way for the A31 roundabout. Clark was a dedicated supporter of the non-conformist Meeting-House which still stands in Meeting-House Lane. Although he lived, worked and worshipped within a very small area of Ringwood, it would be a mistake to assume that Clark's life was confined within its parish boundaries. He had many business links with both London and Poole, and his letters show that he made regular trips to both places. His two daughters, who sadly died in their twenties, were both sent to London to be educated.

Like many of his contemporaries, Clark owned several public houses. He was also a wine and spirits merchant and a dealer in large quantities of iron, all of which he imported through the port of Poole.

Clark died in 1841 a very wealthy and respected man; in his will he left many generous bequests to charities in the town and also to his beloved Meeting House. His name is perpetuated by his most notable and well-known legacy, Clark's Almshouses in the Quomp.

The fifth brewing firm to appear in the 1784 directory of Ringwood was Tunks & Sweetland. Stephen Tunks was an important figure in Ringwood's history and Timothy Sweetland (or Swetland) was a builder who partnered him in several of his enterprises. Their brewery was situated in Christchurch Road and a remnant of it forms part of today's Ringwood Brewery. To the right of the present Brewery shop door can be seen a course of bricks inscribed with the name and date 'Wm. Bramble 1760', though what connection Bramble had with the building is unknown.

At that time the brewery extended over a much larger area right down to the Millstream, on land now occupied by Parkside Industrial Estate. The malthouse was situated in nearby Duck Island Lane. The brewery was one of the oldest and largest in Ringwood. On January 28th 1822, following the death of Mr. Tunks, it was advertised to be let as:

*'A valuable and extensive BREWERY and MALTHOUSE, lately occupied by Mr. Stephen Tunks, in which a very extensive business of a Maltster and Brewer has been carried on for upwards of a century; comprising a Malthouse which will wet 18 to 20 quarters a week and a Brewhouse 40 feet long by 37 feet wide.'*

There were also four very long cellars, barley stores, stables, a combined spirit cellar and cooperage for barrel-making, a counting-house and a skilling [a lean-to or shed] for storing small beer.

The premises were said to be *'very well adapted for any person who may wish to embark in the brewery business, or any brewers desirous of extending their trade, being in a town and neighbourhood where there is a good opening.'* This description could still have applied to the site when Ringwood Brewery decided to move there in 1986, having outgrown their original site at Mintey's Yard.

On the town Tithe Map of 1845 the brewery was shown, with fewer outbuildings, as belonging to John Crutcher. Soon afterwards it became William Munden's ironworks and in 1876 the first site of J.J.Armfield's famous Vale of Avon iron foundry, the originator of Ringwood's modern engineering industry. Now the circle has come full turn - once again it is a brewery, this time with Old Thumper to put Ringwood back on the map!

The earlier brewery's owner, Stephen Tunks, was closely involved in almost every aspect of Ringwood's affairs during the first two decades of the 19th century. Some details of his many activities may help set the story of the brewers against the historical and social background of that time.

Unlike most of his fellow-brewers who were non-conformists, Tunks was a member of the Parish Church, occupying a large enclosed pew in the north gallery of the old church. As such, he was able to hold a number of public offices, particularly Justice of the Peace and Chairman of the Select Vestry, the equivalent of the Parish Council at that time.

In his capacity as magistrate, Stephen Tunks was much involved with plans to combat the threatened invasion by the French during the Napoleonic Wars. By April 1798 invasion appeared imminent and so a meeting was held in Ringwood to collect voluntary contributions towards the defence of the country. A list of subscribers was published in the Salisbury & Winchester Journal. Second only to William Mills Esquire of Bisterne, who contributed 20 guineas, was Stephen Tunks, who gave £20. Even his servants gave two guineas— how heavily were they 'leaned on' to contribute, one wonders? (For the benefit of younger readers, a guinea was £1.1s or £1.05.)

One of Tunks' main duties was to organize the local defence volunteers, raised to defend the neighbourhood should the invasion

TO MALTSTERS AND BREWERS.

TO be LET, and entered upon at Michaelmas next,—All that valuable and extensive BREWERY and MALTHOUSE, situate in the town of RINGWOOD, in the county of Southampton, lately occupied by Mr. Stephen Tunks, in which a very extensive business of a Maltster and Brewer has been carried on for upwards of a century: comprising a Malthouse, which will wet 18 to 20 quarters a week; a Brewhouse, 40 feet long by 37 feet wide; a Shed adjoining the brewhouse for casks, 12 feet long by 37 feet wide; a Cellar, 335 feet long by 20 feet wide, the centre of which is 28 feet wide; another Cellar, 102 feet long by 18 feet wide, with store over for barley; another Cellar, 29 feet wide; a Shed, adjoining ditto, 40 feet long and 10 feet wide; a Stable, 35 feet long and 17 feet wide, with a loft over the same; a Spirit Cellar and Cooperage, in one building, 68 feet long and 16 feet wide, skilling to ditto for small beer; Cellar, 68 feet long and 11 feet wide; a Counting-house with small Cellar adjoining, with other suitable outbuildings and offices.

And also a convenient and commodious DWELLING-HOUSE, with a Garden, Summer-house, and Cold Bath, on the borders of a branch of the River Avon, now occupied by Mr. Peter Vey; and also a piece of Meadow Land, adjoining or near thereto, containing 2 acres or thereabouts, and a large Garden surrounded with a lofty wall; and also another MALTHOUSE, in Ringwood aforesaid, which will wet from 10 to 12 quarters per week, and a Cottage, Garden, and small Paddock adjoining thereto, also late in the occupation of the said Mr. Tunks.

The above will be found very well adapted for any person who may wish to embark in the brewery business, or any brewers desirous of extending their trade, being in a town and neighbourhood where there is a good opening, and the taker will have the opportunity of purchasing or renting a great quantity of well frequented Inns and Public Houses.

For a view of the Premises apply to the respective occupiers; and for further particulars apply, if by letter post-paid, to Mr. R. H. Parr, solicitor, Ringwood.

*January* 18, 1822. [8928

*Print -out of Salisbury Journal*

occur. Tunks himself held the rank of Major; very probably he belonged to a cavalry company, either the South Hants Yeomanry or the Ringwood Light Dragoons. Another two companies of infantry were described at their first full parade thus:

*'August 18th 1798- The two companies of Ringwood Volunteers, clothed in a handsome uniform, marched to church on Sunday last and heard an excellent discourse, appropriate to the occasion, preached by the Rev. Mr.Hawtrey. On Tuesday afternoon they met in the field in their uniform dress, and went through their exercise with great exactness, making a very military appearance, after which the men were regaled with bread, cheese and strong beer; and the ladies of Ringwood were served with tea, cake and wine at a tent erected for that purpose.'*

The surrender of the Dutch fleet, although in hindsight only a minor victory, provided an opportunity for Tunks to demonstrate his rather ostentatious patriotism:

*'September 7th 1799 - The town of Ringwood was on Thursdaynighthandsomely illuminated, particularly the houses of Major Tunks and Captain Oake, the former exhibiting a fine Transparency of Britannia pointing to the names of our most distinguished naval heroes.'*

These illuminations and transparencies were a regular feature of Georgian celebrations in London and other cities, but it may come as a surprise to find that Ringwood also managed such elaborate displays. Candles burning brightly in the windows of the town on a dark night must have made a pretty scene. After the Battle of Trafalgar, Ringwood was again illuminated, with almost every candle blackened on the outside in mourning for Lord Nelson.

Another of Tunks' tasks was the maintenance of law and order. In the days before any regular police force, when the only law enforcement officer was the parish constable, the gentlemen of Ringwood found it necessary to form a group called 'The Ringwood Association'. Meeting at the Crown Inn, its purpose was 'for prosecuting felons and the protection of property'. For example when three horses were stolen in 1798, a guinea reward was offered for each horse returned to the Crown Inn, and five guineas offered by the Association for information leading to the prosecution of the thieves.

Up until 1801, the Crown Inn was situated in the Market Place, being the prominent building next to Church Hatch which is now standing empty. However in that year Stephen Tunks bought the Inn and promptly transferred its licence to its present location at Friday's Cross. This property had previously been licensed as the King's Head, which Tunks in turn transferred to premises in Christchurch Road opposite his brewery.

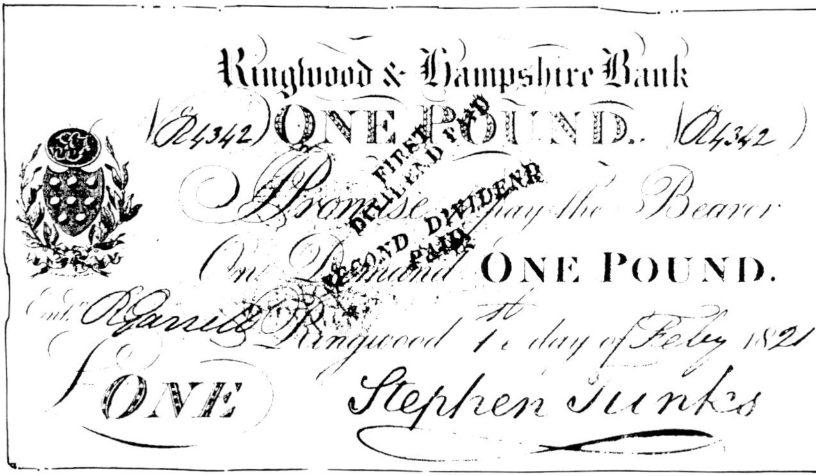


*Tunks Pound Note (by courtesy of the RedHouse Museum Christchurch)* N.T.S.

The old Crown building in the Market Place was turned by Tunks into 'The Ringwood & Hampshire Bank', brewing and banking being a common combination at that period. The bank issued its own bank notes, signed by Tunks personally. One of these banknotes is on display at the Red House Museum, Christchurch, and another at Shering's Museum, Fordingbridge.

It may possibly have been Tunks who added the columned portico, the Venetian window and the mathematical tiles to the facade of the old Crown building. Its imposing central position in the Market Place must thus have reinforced Tunks' own central position in Ringwood society.

Like many other brewers of his time, Tunks owned a string of tied-houses, just as today Ringwood Brewery owns 'The Inn on the Furlong' in Meeting House Lane and 'Old Thumper' in Bournemouth. As well as the Crown and the King's Head, Tunks owned the Fish, the Lamb, the Rose & Crown, the Smiths Arms and the Globe. He also possessed several more outside Ringwood but there is no doubt that it was the Crown which was his principal inn.

Under Tunks' ownership, the new Crown Inn flourished and became the headquarters of many of his activities. Its first landlord, James Lindsey, remained until 1808, when John King took over. Did the locals make a pun of King gaining the Crown? It was during King's time as landlord, that Tunks began his 'Subscription Balls'. For a season's subscription the gentry and well-to-do townsfolk enjoyed regular balls held at the Crown's Assembly Rooms:

*'April 20th 1812- The Subscription Ball at the Crown Inn Ringwood on Thursday last was numerously attended, dancing was kept up with great spirit till a very late hour. The politeness of the stewards, aided by the attraction of Baker's excellent band, had caused the rooms to be crowded to excess, to obviate the like inconvenience in future Stephen Tunks Esq. announced his intention of building spacious ball and card rooms previous to the next season; which have long been a desideration for the accommodation of so populous and respectable a neighbourhood. Upwards of 50 new subscribers were obtained on Mr. Tunks intention being known.'*

Part of these new rooms may be what is today called 'Squire's Room'; it is interesting that as long ago as those Regency days it was felt there was a need for a larger hall in 'populous and respectable' Ringwood!

In 1814 the Crown was the venue for the local branch of the Society for the Propagation of Christian Knowledge, of which Tunks was a founder member. He also chaired a meeting there to petition Parliament to effect the entire abolition of slavery, which obtained 'a vast number of signatures.'

When peace was declared it was celebrated in Ringwood in magnificent style, recalling the days of old England at its merriest:

*June 18th 1814 - 'Thursday last was a great day of great festivity at the loyal town of Ringwood. The inhabitants came forward with a liberal subscription in order to make the poor man's heart rejoice - a very fine ox having been purchased, it was dressed by the bakers of the town who got the whole completely ready by two o'clock with a large quantity of plum pudding, vegetables etc. Arrangements were made for the dinner in Bickerley Common, and at two o'clock the sound of the bugle horn and the firing of cannon announced it ready, when near one thousand people sat down and partook of John Bull's Old English fare, good beef, plum pudding and excellent strong beer.'*

July 17th 1814 - *'Inhabitants assembled on Wednesday evening to witness a grand display of fire-works on Bickerley Common. On Thursday morning peace was proclaimed through the town in a grand and solemn manner; besides the usual procession the members of the Friendly Society, with their band and colours, attended; the trumpet sounded before each reading, after which the band played God Save the King, and three huzzas were given. In the evening the town seemed in a blaze, the whole being beautifully illuminated; transparencies and devices were to be seen at almost every house, and the multitude that crowded the streets on this most auspicious event was immense. On Friday evening there was a ball at the Crown Inn, which was numerously attended by the ladies and gentlemen of the town and its vicinity.'*

The next year Charles Russell became the new tenant of the Crown. By this time its coaching days were in full swing, with the Portsmouth & Plymouth coach changing horses at noon for Portsmouth and at 3p.m. for Exeter and Plymouth every day.

Following Napoleon's escape from Elba, war broke out again but was finally ended at the Battle of Waterloo. The first anniversary of this victory was again celebrated at the Crown:

'June 20th 1816 - *The gentlemen at Ringwood had a most sumptuous dinner at the Crown Inn on Tuesday last in celebration of the ever-memorable victory at Waterloo. Every delicacy of the season was served up in great style by Mr.Russell and the company, amongst whom the greatest possible harmony prevailed, did not break up till a late hour.'*

In 1817 the men of Ringwood had another cause for celebration when they beat Lyndhurst in what could be Ringwood's first game of cricket to be recorded in detail. No doubt Ringwood ale flowed freely after the game, which was almost certainly played on the Bickerley. There were only two men in each team, in what was apparently a single-wicket match:

'September 27th 1817 - *On Wednesday last a match at cricket which had excited much interest was played at Ringwood between Messrs Lainson and Neale, two first rate players from Lyndhurst, and Messrs Martin and Warne of Ringwood, which was decided in favour of the latter, as appears by the following correct statement of the game -*

| Ringwood | | | | |
|---|---|---|---|---|
| | 1st inn. | | 2nd inn. | |
| Martin | b. Neale | 10 | b.Lainson | 12 |
| Warne | leg before wicket | 8 | ditto | 4 |
| | | Total 18 | | Total 16 |
| Lyndhurst | | | | |
| Neale | b. Martin | 2 | b. Martin | 5 |
| Lainson | ditto | 0 | ditto | 1 |
| | | Total 2 | | Total 6 |

Majority in favour of Ringwood 26'

In 1820 the Crown was the scene of some lively electioneering by one of the two parliamentary candidates for Hampshire. Only male free-holders with property valued at £2 per annum were entitled to vote for these 'knights of the shire', nevertheless the whole town seems to have enjoyed the occasion:

March 11th 1820 - *'On Thursday evening last John Fleming Esq., one of the candidates for the county, was drawn into the town of Ringwood by the inhabitants to the Crown Inn, where he slept. On alighting, he ordered a hogshead of strong beer to be given to the populace and presented the ringers with two guineas. The following morning he was again drawn by the inhabitants a mile out of the town.'*

Perhaps if politicians of today were still allowed to buy beer for the populace they would be more likely to be received with similar enthusiasm!

Life, however, was often anything but merry for many poorer people. The long years of war were followed by a period of high bread prices and low wages for the farm labourers, many of whom had been depossessed of their lands following the Enclosure Acts. When a cold spell of weather brought extra severe hardship to these people, Tunks was among those wealthy gentlemen who considered it their Christian duty to dispense charity, which relieved the symptoms but did little to change the causes of this poverty:

February 12th 1820 - *'A subscription, under the patronage of our worthy vicar, was generously supported by Lord Fitzharris, H.Baring, W.Mills, J.Morant, S.Tunks and W.Tice Esqrs. with numerous other gentlemen, to the amount of nearly £200. Beef, soup, peas and fuel have been distributed to the poor twice a week at very reduced prices.'*

The grimmer side of life during this period can also be illustrated by the following account of a horrific crime connected with Tunks' brewery which shook the whole of Ringwood in 1820:

**'ATROCIOUS MURDER**

*- On Sunday the 31st July about six o'clock in the morning, a very poor man upwards of sixty years of age, named James Tilly, was found murdered, and thrown into the River Avon about 200 yards from the town of Ringwood. The inhabitants of the place were at a loss to conjecture the cause for which the perpetrators had committed the horrid deed, Tilly being a very inoffensive man, who scarcely ever had a farthing in his pocket; he had in fact received parochial relief for many years. It appeared that he had been used in a most shocking manner, having received very severe blows on the head, breast, loins, shoulders, back*

*and face; one of his eyes was beaten out of the socket and lay on his cheek. It evidently appeared too, that the poor fellow's throat had been severely pressed, so as to cause strangulation. The following morning at nine o'clock Mr.Charles Harbin, the Coroner for the hundred of Ringwood, held an inquest on the body and at twelve o'clock noon adjourned till eight in the evening; during which time it was discovered that the brewhouse belonging to Stephen Tunks Esq had been broken open, and two casks of butter, weighing 144lbs stolen. The footsteps of some persons were traced from the brewhouse in a direct line towards the river where the poor man was found; and it is generally believed that those people who broke open and robbed the brewery met the old man on their way (with their booty) and to prevent a discovery put an end to his existence in the cruel manner above stated. The inquiry was renewed at eight o'clock in the evening, and a verdict of 'Wilful Murder' was returned against some person or persons unknown. A strong suspicion having fallen on persons near the town, warrants were granted, and a diligent search was made, but nothing has yet been found to lead to a discovery.'*

A case for Sherlock Holmes if ever there was one! But as this occurred in the days long before any kind of systematic detection, either fictional or real, the crime was never satisfactorily solved. Who were the persons near the town who were strongly suspected? Were they a group of gypsies who were blamed for every wrongdoing?

The sequel to this tale seems almost ludicrous. In March 1821 a Ringwood woman named Sarah Whiffin was tried at Winchester Assizes for the murder of James Tilly. She was acquitted on the grounds of insanity, which was clearly proved by several witnesses, particularly the surgeon of the gaol, Mr. Lyford. (This must surely be the same Dr. Lyford who had attended Jane Austen on her deathbed in Winchester four years earlier - a curious link between the famous novelist and one of Ringwood's long-forgotten nobodies!)

If the evidence as stated was correct, it seems extremely improbable that this woman could single-handedly have beaten and strangled Tilly, thrown him in the river and carried away two casks weighing 144lbs! It would appear that the authorities were merely looking for a scapegoat, and so poor half-witted Sarah, the mother of two illegitimate children claiming parish relief, became almost as much a victim as the murdered man.

The two casks of butter mentioned in the robbery are intriguing - what were they doing in the brewhouse? It is unlikely this was a misprint for 'bitter' as the casks were given in weight, not capacity. Probably it will remain, like the rest of the crime, a mystery.

Shortly afterwards on Thursday 28th June 1821, Stephen Tunks died, aged either 76 according to the burial registers, or 72 according to the inscription on his solitary tombstone, which can still be discovered to the west of the church porch.

A week later notice was given that in consequence of a deficiency which had been discovered in his assets, all payments at his Ringwood & Hampshire Bank were suspended. Exactly why the bank failed is not certain; possibly Tunks had been using bank deposits to cover up deficits in his brewery. This may, however, be doing Tunks an injustice for following a series of financial crises, private banks were failing throughout the country.

Nevertheless this was not the first occasion that there had been problems. In 1807 a case involving Tunks' bank had been the centre of much speculation:

'Winchester March 7th 1807 - *Great interest was excited by the expected trial of W.Jones, late Clerk in the Bank of Tunks & Swetland at Ringwood, committed on a charge of having forged a bill of exchange for £55 and likewise charged on suspicion with having broke open the bank of his employers and plundered it of notes and cash to the amount of more than £3400, but this prosecution was dropped, and Jones was of course discharged.'*

No reason was given why the charge was dropped - forgery was then a capital offence and £3400 an enormous amount of money to have 'gone missing'. In view of subsequent events, a large question mark must hang over this whole suspicious episode.

The 1821 failure of the bank came as a great blow to its customers, including the Parish Church, which had entrusted all the parish money with Tunks. The Church was responsible for all sorts of financial fundings, particularly the allocation of the Poor Relief, so emergency measures had to be taken. Another firm of bankers, Hicks & White, advanced £600 until a new parish rate could be levied.

*Tunk's Bank early this century*

A further casualty was William Clark, who wrote to a colleague, *'The death of Mr. Tunks and the unfortunate disarrangement of his affairs have caused a gloom in this place, and having a balance on his books due to me which is now locked up, I should take it a great favour if you would remit me £70.7.4d.'*

It was Clark who filed the suit of bankruptcy against Tunks in the High Court of Chancery in an effort to recoup his money. It took many years to sort out, during which time Tunks' widow lived on at the Market Place property until it was finally auctioned off in 1827 along with other assets.

In sharp contrast to Clark, who is remembered as probably the most generous benefactor Ringwood has ever known, the financial difficulties that Tunks bequeathed to the parish have cast a cloud of notoriety over his memory. His once unblemished reputation as successful brewer, trusted administrator, loyal patriot, Christian benefactor and social king-pin of Ringwood is forever tarnished by the unhappy consequences of his death.

The death of Tunks could be said to mark the beginning of the end for the Ringwood brewers. Several factors for their gradual decline have already been mentioned: the change in people's drinking habits and tastes, the influence of the temperance movement, the acquisition of the smaller breweries by larger ones from outside the locality, and the use of their sites for other purposes. As Poole and the Newfoundland trade declined, a lucrative outlet was lost, and the importance of Ringwood itself waned as Bournemouth grew. The coming of the railway to Ringwood in 1847 also made significant changes, as fewer travellers on horseback, waggons and coaches stopped for refreshment on journeys by road. It became easy for breweries in larger towns to acquire tied-houses in Ringwood and supply them by rail.

All this may be seen by some as progress, but no doubt many local people must have regretted the loss of their favourite Ringwood brew and hankered after the return of the 'good old days'!

## CONCLUSION

So what, you may ask, is the point of all these stories of people who now lay dead and buried for over 150 years? Hopefully this booklet may help people to appreciate the efforts of past generations of townsfolk and to value more fully the heritage they have handed down to us.

Perhaps when you are next in the Market Place on Market Day you may pause to imagine William Clark examining his samples of barley by the old church wall, watched by Stephen Tunks from the steps of his bank. As you walk down West Street you may picture a horse-drawn dray pulling out of Carter's brewery past the aproned landlord of the Antelope Inn, or almost hear a post-horn signalling the arrival into town of a mail-coach from the west.

Times - and Ringwood - have changed enormously since those days. Tunks would be amazed that his old adversaries, the French, come as visitors and that Ringwood is now twinned with the French town of Pont Audemer. The railway has come and gone. Clark, with his problems of waggon deliveries from Kent, would be astonished that lorries can now travel the distance in a matter of hours. Whatever would he make of the A31? What would be Miss Carter's reaction if she were to know that her philanthropic gift to the town, the Lecture Hall, had been demolished to make way for a 1960's shop and office block?

So much of what these people knew and loved has been swept away. Yet despite the huge alterations in the size and character of Ringwood, some aspects of the old town would remain just recognisable to them.

The market, though much changed in character since the days when corn and cattle were the principal commodities sold, is still held in the Market Place every Wednesday. The Meeting-House has been saved from demolition and still overlooks the Furlong, even though what was always a green pasture is now the main car park! Bickerley Common has been obtained by the Town Council and is still used on special occasions for town celebrations.

These places have long associations with the community of Ringwood and no doubt our predecessors would approve of their continued use. But perhaps the brewers would derive greatest pleasure from knowing that Ringwood beer, which in their day achieved such high level of popularity, is now once again renowned throughout the country.

So next time you down a pint of Ringwood ale, spare a thought for the brewers of old Ringwood and raise your glass in a toast to their memory!

**References**

All the advertisement details and news reports unless stated otherwise have been extracted from the Salisbury and Winchester Journal of the given date. Otherwise evidence has come from the following documents held at Hampshire Record Office.

Documents relating to Carter's Brewery - HRO Ref 20M80
Microfilm M139 E/T25,27,30,34

The will of Joseph Veal Jnr - HRO Ref llM61/17

The letter-books & accounts of William Clark HRO Ref llM61/56-60

Documents of Star Lane Brewery- HRO Ref llM61/9-15/18/20/161

The will of Joseph Fryer HRO Ref llM61/280

Bastardy Order concerning Sarah Whiffin HRO Ref 22M84 PO113a/96

Pigot's Directory 1830

Sadler's Directory 1784 - Hampshire Record Office

Ringwood Parish and Non-conformist Registers transcribed by Dr Little

**Bibliography**


| | |
|---|---|
| Cross D. | The Story of Ringwood's Industries (1964) |
| Filmer R. | Hops and Hop Picking (1982) |
| Handcock W.G. | Soe longe as there comes noe women (1989) |
| Keppel R. | Ringwood Ales (unpublished, written c.1958) |
| Kingsbury A.H | The History of Ringwood (1894) |
| Little R.H. | The History of the Brewing Industry of Ringwood (unpublished. Written 1966) |
| Lovett M. | Brewing and Breweries (1981) |
| Monckton H.A. | A History of Beer & Ale (1966) |
| Murray A.J.H. | Trinity Church 1781-1981 (1981) |
| & others | |